Who is McKenzie?

Peter Stanway

Copyright © 2011 by Peter Stanway

ISBN 0-9839186-4-3

ISBN13 978-0-9839186-4-6

Library of Congress Control Number: 2011944753

Printed in the United States of America

RevMedia Publishing
Po Box 5172
Kingwood, TX 77325
USA

A division of Revelation Ministries

www.revmediapublishing.com
www.revministries.com
www.revmedianetwork.com
www.revmediatv.com

Cover design by Peter Stanway

To contact Peter Stanway: www.peterstanwaybooks.com

See inside back page for more details.

DEDICATION

To every McKenzie both lost and found....

TABLE OF CONTENTS

INTRODUCTION

This first book in the *'McKenzie'* series serves to introduce us to this remarkable character; we travel the globe and enter into the fascinating world of McKenzie. It gives us an overview of his enthralling life. McKenzie is intriguing, upright, fearful but hopeful......The truth is that there is a bit of McKenzie in all of us and a bit of all of us in McKenzie.

As his story unfolds, the pieces fit together like a jig-saw and a picture builds as we get to know McKenzie. In an intriguing and breath-taking diversity of adventures McKenzie dodges in and out of a world that's full of evil, he goes through a plethora of deeply spiritual experiences; some amazingly good and others frighteningly bad.

Championing the cause for C.A.N.T. (Campaign Against Nuclear Terror) leads McKenzie into many dangerous and clandestine meetings. The characters he meets weave in and out of his fascinating life but, ultimately, where will it all lead?

Page by page we are captivated and left feeling hungry for more. Not only are we questioning what will happen to McKenzie but we are faced with the same life-changing questions that we ourselves must answer....

The absorbing and mysterious McKenzie stories will appeal to a wide range of people from diverse cultures and countries. Everyone will identify in some way with him, but just who is McKenzie?

1

McKenzie Confronts His Fears

The air was so humid that McKenzie's cheap off-the-shelf spectacles slid down the greasy slope of his aristocratic aquiline nose. Almost habitually and certainly without thinking, he pushed them back up to the bridge of his nose where beads of sweat formed between his furrowing eyebrows.

At any cost, McKenzie was determined to finish his paper that he would present that afternoon to the scientific intelligentsia at the World Summit for Unilateral Disarmament in Sao Paulo, Brazil.

For a moment he was distracted. Was that a creak he heard on the well-worn stairway outside of his shabby hotel room or was his fertile mind playing tricks on him.....?

McKenzie smiled inwardly, why was he anxious? His mind went back to the time when, as an eight year old boy, he woke up during the night struggling to make sense of the worst technicolour nightmare he had ever had.

His pyjamas stuck to him with sweat, his eyes, bulging, stared wildly into the unyielding darkness that surrounded him. His heart was racing so fast that it felt like it would burst out of his chest. Fear paralysed his throat as he struggled to scream out, 'Dad!'

'What is it son?'. The strong, reassuring sound of his dad's voice pierced the darkness and dissolved McKenzie's fears....

2

McKenzie Makes a Difference

McKenzie stared blankly at the grotesque panorama of chaos and poverty that spread out before him. The rank smell of decay nauseated him. What could he do? Where could he start?

Njenga slum was home to around one million displaced and marginalised inhabitants on the edge of Nairobi, Kenya. Looking at the impossible task that confronted him, McKenzie remembered the story his father had told him when he was a boy.

Another boy, around the same age a McKenzie, was walking along a beach as the tide was going out. The shoreline was littered with flotsam and jetsam from the previous night's violent storm. In among the debris were hundreds of dying starfish.

The boy stooped to pick up a starfish and gently threw it back into the deeper water. As he went on his way, he continued to pick up starfish at random and throw them also into the sea. An older man, who was likewise out for a stroll, saw what the boy was doing and gruffly remarked that there were too many starfish to save, the task was impossible and the young boy would be as well to give up.

'What difference can you make?' he quizzed. ' I may not be able to make a difference to all of them but I can certainly make a difference to the ones I put back into the ocean!'

McKenzie's mind was made up. He would start with one person in the slums and aim to make a difference. One-by-one, he would try to help as many as he could....

3

McKenzie Meets Seduction

The heavy rain beat steadily down on the cathedral steps, turning the dust to mud and then washing it away. Spain in the rain – not what he was hoping for! McKenzie sat under the canopy of a café situated on one side of a very beautiful plaza and thoughtfully sipped his café con leche. Normally, he would have savoured this moment while indulging in his favourite pastime: people watching, but the cobbled plaza, now shiny and treacherous, was almost deserted.

McKenzie focussed on the drenched horse-drawn open carriage that waited in vain for tourists. Statuesque, the chestnut brown mare stood completely immobile seeming to enjoy this welcome respite and happily unaware of the unseasonably bad weather. Sun-beaten, the gypsy driver sat forlornly wrapped in a brightly coloured thin plastic poncho that caught the drips from his sodden stiff brimmed hat that, in turn, sheltered the permanent 'Ducados' cigarette burning slowly between his sardonic silent lips.

Would she keep their appointment? Was he bothered? McKenzie had developed an inherent trust in God that gave him the confidence to believe that no matter what happened, everything would work out for the best. Was he bothered? Not at all. However, when Maria Lopez de las Flores appeared out of a narrow lane on the other side of the square, his heart did skip a beat. There was an air of elegance and sophistication, like twin sisters, that accompanied Maria wherever she went.

McKenzie scrutinised every inch of her as she made her way towards him. Her jet-black hair was tightly pulled back from her pale sculptured face. Her dark eyes, like mysterious deep pools and her ever-so-slightly pouting red lips, perfectly complimenting her crimson-red shawl meticulously draped from her pushed-back shoulders, like a proud matador's cape after the kill. She exuded confidence. He was going to have to tread very carefully with this one.

He stood to his feet as she approached. Maria locked her hazel eyes on McKenzie's Aryan-blue stare. Her delicately perfumed hand hovered gracefully in front of McKenzie as she waited to be greeted. He bowed slowly and taking her hand gently in his, he kissed the back of it,

'Charmed' said McKenzie, smiling broadly. 'Thank you for coming'.
'The pleasure is all mine.' Maria's melodious voice resonated from deep within her like a treasure that had been hidden until now. Her teeth sparkled although there was no sun. She radiated her own light.

'Steady…' mused McKenzie, convinced that Maria could read his thoughts…..

4

McKenzie Meets His Past

His MP4 player was out of juice, so McKenzie tuned into the noise that surrounded him. He zoned into private conversations until he found something that interested him. He was back in Scotland, in Glasgow, in a massive shopping mall that had sprung-up from nowhere since his last visit. Malls are noisy places and they are fascinating.

Nameless people, thousands of them, milled around in all directions. Every one of them had a unique story to tell….McKenzie knew that all they wanted was someone to listen. He pondered this as he sipped his Starbucks latte, casually eavesdropping into whatever conversation caught his attention in the ambience.

"Hello son, is this seat taken?" McKenzie followed the voice to a smartly dressed old man with piercing blue eyes and a recently done neat haircut. He was holding a mug of tea standing in front of the empty seat at McKenzie's table.

"No, it's yours", smiled McKenzie politely.

"Thank you. Busy place, isn't it?""Yes", responded McKenzie. "My name's Archie, what's your name?" As he cordially stretched-out his hand towards McKenzie.

"McKenzie's my name", he said as he warmly shook Archie's hand.
"McKenzie? That's a great Scottish name, a name to be proud of. Where are you from McKenzie?"

"Originally from up north, the Outer Hebrides."

"What part? I was stationed there during the war."

"A wee island called Scalpay, just off Harris."

"Scalpay!" exclaimed Archie. "My first love came from Scalpay. You must know her, Moira McLeod?"

McKenzie was taken aback, almost everyone on Scalpay was from the McLeod clan.

"When was that?" asked McKenzie respectfully. "Och, I was just a boy, seventeen years old. Moira was only sixteen."

McKenzie quickly did the math. This happened around seventy years ago, putting Archie in his eighties. He remembered that he had an aunty Moira, his dad's sister. But surely, it couldn't be her….?

5

McKenzie and the Waiter

Maria sat down on the vacant seat at McKenzie's table, her back as straight as a poker. The slim good-looking waiter, no more than a boy, arrived instantly and slowly eyed Maria up and down. He deliberately licked his lips and almost imperceptibly pushed out his still-forming hips in Maria's direction.

'Por favor', said McKenzie, unheard. Coughing far too loudly, he said it again.

'Perdóneme', the waiter said abstractly not taking his eyes off Maria's pursed lips.

'Dos cafes con leche', said McKenzie, obviously annoyed at the distinct lack of attention he was being given. 'Ahora mismo', said the boy with the voice of a trained Hollywood actor as he drifted off in slow-motion into the café. If it was a movie, the camera would have cut from the waiter to a close-up of Maria's captivating face, her eyelids dropping coyly to conceal a delicate blush on her impeccable cheeks, then dissolving into a misty filter and cut.

However, this was not a movie set per se, it was every inch real life and in this seduction race it was neck-and-neck between Maria and the waiter. The question was: who was the seducer and who was being seduced?

The whole scenario made McKenzie sick to the pit of his stomach. If he could have been anywhere else, he would have. Right now there was a job to be done. McKenzie had to delicately extract the information he had been sent to obtain and deliver it, post-haste, to his employers.

6

McKenzie is Spared

Condensation stuck to the window like mist on a Scottish mountain. However, McKenzie was not in Scotland, he was in South East Asia, Myanmar to be precise, Mandalay City to be exact.

A drop of water left its trail and through the window blurred images of the city made indistinct shapes through the glass. McKenzie was only wearing a t-shirt and bermuda shorts but they were soaked through with sweat. He was alone for the moment but his head was still spinning from what had just happened.

The tiny, plain room had been packed with around fifty people praying. Prayers like McKenzie had never heard; loud, fervent and passionate. Almost everyone had been weeping, their faces streaked with tears, crying out to God.

Suddenly the bamboo door had burst open and at least twenty policemen brandishing clubs had rushed in. It was carnage. The sickening thuds on beating flesh, breaking bones and frenzied screaming now filled the room that had just moments before been filled with the sound of prayer.

Blood was splattered across the walls and ceiling. The illegal church was effectively stopped and the Christians were dragged out traumatised and in shock and roughly thrown into the waiting paddy wagons.

McKenzie had pushed himself into a corner squatting. He waited for the blows but they never came. As abruptly as the militia came in, they left. McKenzie was bewildered. Had the enforcers been blinded? How could they have missed him? Surely it was a miracle…..

7

McKenzie Feels His Age

As McKenzie sat waiting in the car, his feet turned to blocks of ice. Even though it was minus fourteen degrees Celsius outside, he couldn't remember the cold weather affecting him this much. Maybe he was simply getting older and with each passing year the cold penetrated deeper into his bones.

McKenzie didn't like to think of himself as getting old. He still felt young at heart and his memories of bygone days were as vivid as the day they happened. He hated the cold weather and day-dreamed of the times he had lived in hotter countries.

In truth, McKenzie *was* getting older. He wasn't an old man although he struggled to do the things he used to. He was unfit. Maybe if he exercised he would feel younger, but the thought of all that hard work exhausted him just thinking about it! However, he owed it to himself and he owed it to the people who depended on him. He felt guilty about his lack of responsibility. He resolved to do better in the future…..

What was keeping her? He sighed and his breath turned to vapour. He decided to get out of the car in order to stand up and straighten his legs. Instantly, the frost attacked his ears and nose and thoughts of frostbite invaded his mind.

There was nothing else for it; he would have to go for a brisk walk in an attempt to get his circulation going. He couldn't go far because, as yet, he was unfamiliar with Moscow and its ways. Of one thing, however, he was adamant; as soon as he could, he would buy himself a furry *ushanka* to keep his head and ears warm!

The sound of a car back-firing instinctively made McKenzie spin around. There were no cars to be seen. At once, his eyes were drawn to the crumpled shape of his contact, Helga, lying just ten metres away, face-down in yesterday's snow. A crimson pool of blood oozed from underneath her, melting the snow in a sinister path towards him……

8

McKenzie Gets High

The air at such altitude, in the foothills of the Himalayas, was incredibly thin and dry making it impossible to sweat despite the scorching heat. McKenzie's blood pressure was far too high causing his face to flush like a beetroot. His pulse was beating so hard that he thought his head would explode and his heart would burst.

The journey to Khoplang, a tiny village in the district of Gorkha, took two days walking. Much of the dirt road had been washed away by the frequent torrential rains making it heavy-going under foot for McKenzie and his Sherpa guide.

Wading through the river in full spate was not an option, even although it would have cut hours off the journey. When the driver of an old truck offered them a lift, McKenzie and his guide jumped at the chance despite the exorbitant price they had to pay for the privilege.

McKenzie had an important meeting with, Chitra, the Chief Elder of the village. Chitra had some valuable information that may just expose the Communist insurgents' take-over of the former kingdom of Nepal. Their sweep had already started when they raped and pillaged their way towards Kathmandu.

After the King had been deposed, the Communists had coerced their way to becoming part of the hastily formed coalition government. Since then Nepal had progressively regressed into austerity with the people struggling to eat and stay warm.

Was it possible to stop their wave of terror?....

9

McKenzie's Reality Check

It started as a tiny speckle in the far, far distance, in the macro-space behind McKenzie's eyes. Sitting in his recliner easy-chair soaking up the sunshine through the window of his bedroom, he almost purred like a pussy-cat.

McKenzie inclined his head towards the wall and watched the shifting shadows and dancing lights that were refracted through the trees from the garden outside. A cloud momentarily passed in front of the sun bringing McKenzie back from day-dreaming to the stark reality of the matter in hand: why was Helga murdered and who did it?

He had no option but to walk away the night she was killed. To get involved with a murder would have complicated everything. He had been waiting on Helga returning with a contact name; a name that would take him to the leader of the Unilateral

Disarmament Movement in Russia. Whoever killed Helga didn't want McKenzie to have that name.

McKenzie knew that this was more, much more, than a group of Ban the Bomb ex-hippie protesters. He wondered if he was getting in too deep…..

The sun came back out and McKenzie allowed himself the luxury of letting his mind drift off to more pleasant places. He could hear his mother's voice calling him from far away…..

10

McKenzie Listens Hard

McKenzie sat sipping his piping-hot mint tea. There wasn't too much tea in the small chunky tumbler on account of it being crammed full of fresh mint leaves and far too much sugar. He sat at a wobbly table surrounded by a assortment of leathery faced, deeply browned and near toothless men who all looked, at least, twice their age.

They babbled away in a thick Arabic dialect to make sure they kept their conversation secret from uninvited ears. Sucking habitually on their shared hookah pipe, they took no notice of McKenzie's curious gaze.

Marrakech, nestled into the foothills of the snow-capped Atlas Mountains in southern Morocco, is a bizarre place. Sitting at this shabby little café, McKenzie had a commanding view over Djema el Fna, the main square of the old city.

Everywhere he looked, McKenzie could feast his eyes on a vast array of extraordinary delights. Alive with the buzz of tourists and locals alike, the square was a hive of activity day and night. There was never any shortage of fascinating entertainment.

Despite the huge diversity of acts to watch, and tempting food to eat, there was one particular activity that captured McKenzie's undivided attention: the storyteller. Like a talking newspaper from the High Atlas, these specially trained and skilled orators came into the city every few months to tell their news. More popular than the snake-charmers, acrobats and fire-eaters, the crowds flocked to glean news of their distant relatives who lived secluded among the nomadic Berbers.

McKenzie was especially interested in news of Kahina; a young noblewoman who was betrothed to a ruthless Lord of the Atlas, a survivor from the infamous House of Glaoua.

He strained his ears to hear. Although the swelling crowd was hushed and hanging on every word, he still found it challenging to follow the strong Tamazight accent. Suddenly, like the sound of a finger-flick on a pure crystal glass, her name hung in the air resonating above the dusty crowd. It was as he had feared, Kahina was pregnant….

11

McKenzie is Searching

The trees, limp and heavy after days of incessant rainfall, hung silently in the eerie stillness. The inky black sky seemed to crack open for the briefest of moments and a full moon slid out from behind a slow moving invisible cloud spilling light over the forest floor like a tremendous symphony of chiaroscuro.

Bright beams cut through the dense canopy and splashed pools of iridescence onto the damp, thick foliage of the wild forest floor. A magnificent cathedral of majestic Kapok Trees stood frozen, all-too-briefly in time, for the single strobe of the moon's glare as it flashed in the darkness.

Would they ever find what they were looking for…..?

A trickle of sweat slowly made its way down McKenzie's rigid spine. He could trace its course. Beads of perspiration congregated on his furrowed brow. The humidity was tangible. It was two o'clock in the morning and McKenzie longed for the secret solitude of his humble camp-bed back at the hut he fondly called home.

What was he doing lost in the merciless undergrowth of the Amazonian Rainforest? Why was he searching for someone he barely knew?

The child had vanished almost thirty-six hours ago. McKenzie's hand had shot up without his permission when the police officer made an appeal for volunteers. It could have been his little niece who was missing….it could have been him. His mind drifted back to a time when he snuggled into his mother's lap and, with his eyes closed, his mum stroked his hair as she told him this story from the bible…..

"Suppose one of you has a hundred sheep and loses one of them. Doesn't he leave the ninety-nine in the open country and go

after the lost sheep until he finds it? And when he finds it, he joyfully puts it on his shoulders and goes home. Then he calls his friends and neighbours together and says, 'Rejoice with me; I have found my lost sheep.' (Luke 15:3-6).

12

McKenzie Looks for a Connection

McKenzie found himself at church. It was somewhere in middle England at the beginning of spring. With new life bursting out all around him, it seemed like an excellent time to make a God connection in the hope of getting things off to a good start after his winter of isolation.

From the outside it didn't look like a church building. It was a factory unit on an industrial estate. McKenzie liked that. One thing that repulsed McKenzie was overt religion. Non-religious Christianity was often difficult to find. Religion soiled true Christianity like a bad stain. Sadly, it was McKenzie's experience that religion and Christianity were bed-fellows that were difficult to separate.

McKenzie was made to feel welcome when he entered. Without much ado, he progressed into the main auditorium just as the band began to play and they were good. The presentation was good, the sound quality was good, the stage lighting was good and the projected visuals were also good. In fact, to quote the Bible...*they were very good.*

However, as the meeting progressed, the well rehearsed format morphed into a less inspired formula. It was all quite slick, but it was also frustratingly familiar. The potential was there to make this a momentous, life-changing moment for everyone; but religious ritual, cleverly cloaked in charismatic exuberance, sucked at McKenzie's energy. Instead of the tangible presence of God's glory, religion descended like a thick fog.

Many of McKenzie's most amazing life-altering encounters with God had happened outside of the traditional church setting. Now, his attention span wavered and he began to be distracted. He looked around and saw that the congregation were, for the most part, sincere and responsive. The Pastor was sincere. He obviously loved God, the Bible and his flock.

Clearly, he was looking for ways to inspire his people with the fullness of his message, so that, they would have their own personal revelation of what God was saying to each of them.

McKenzie felt the Pastor's frustration and hoped that he would accomplish what he had set out to do. His job was not enviable, it was jolly hard work. He showed great endurance and perseverance. However, it seemed that the beloved would need to be wooed for a while longer…..

13

McKenzie Sets His Face Like Flint

The biting wind and driving rain stung McKenzie's stubbly face. He found it exhilarating and smiled inwardly. Dressed for the weather, he leaned into the brewing storm.

'Bring it on', he said unheard, 'I'm ready!'

McKenzie had been humiliated by his peers. Initially, he was cut to the core and angry. As he planned the most diabolical revenge imaginable, a thought, seemingly from nowhere, popped into his mind. It stopped him in his tracks and he began to feel guilty about his violent and heinous machinations.

Surely there was another way? By reacting out of his hurt feelings he was revealing how much he had been wounded and offended. However, by not reacting but instead adopting a stoic shield of apparent unaffectedness, he would turn the table on the perpetrators.

He prayed to himself silently and asked God to help him. He remembered something he had read from the book of Isaiah:

'Because the Sovereign LORD helps me, I will not be disgraced. Therefore have I set my face like flint, and I know I will not be put to shame.' (Isaiah 50:7)

That was the answer! He put on his bravest face and, like the crags of his beloved Scotland, he would weather this personal storm, seemingly, none the worse for wear….

14

McKenzie Visits the Fourth Dimension

McKenzie found himself caught-up in worship. He had begun to pray in a spontaneous way, but before long, joy and excitement began to well up inside him. All at once it spilled out his mouth in a cascade of words that were not his own.

McKenzie had heard about this and he had read about it. It was even mentioned in the Bible. The words came from deep inside him yet McKenzie began to have an understanding of what he was saying. He began to pray with the same effervescent joy in his own language, English.

As McKenzie continued to pray, in and out of his new language and his own native language, his spirit soared within him. He was transported to another place.

His own voice was no longer his focus of attention. Now, his focus shifted to Jesus, and as he continued he began to see Him in glorious detail. McKenzie's heart pounded and he was alive with tingling joy. Details began to appear: Jesus was smiling, His eyes were ablaze with deep compassion and immense love.

What was happening was real but it was also supernatural. As if McKenzie was experiencing it in another dimension, a fourth dimension. For as long as this time lasted McKenzie was with Jesus, locked in an intimate encounter.

As this experience of true worship came to an end, (after how long he had no idea), McKenzie became aware of his familiar surroundings. He felt exhilarated, overwhelmed, very privileged and blessed....

15

McKenzie is Captured

Bubbles broke the surface then drifted away on the ebb tide as the weighted body sank silently out of sight to the Mediterranean Sea bed forty metres below. Back on the shore in La Carihuela, Miguel and his crew prepared their nets for a full night's fishing....

*   *   *

McKenzie sat gagged and bound, tied to a chair on the deck of Don Pedro Dominguez's luxury yacht, 'La Dama de la Noche'. He had watched the whole scenario unfold. Paco, the Columbian overseer, had walked into a trap and fifty kilos of pure cocaine had been seized by the Columbian authorities.

In the ensuing shoot-out, Paco had managed to escape with only minor injuries. Don Pedro made arrangements for his safe passage to Marbella in Southern Spain. After interrogation at the hands of his henchmen, Don Pedro then ordered his execution. Paco's lifeless body, suitably weighted to make it sink and stay sunk, was tossed overboard; naked and cut to attract and feed the sharks that lived in those clear blue waters.

McKenzie was a 'guest' on 'La Dama de la Noche', at the invitation of Maria de las Flores who had lured him into Don Pedro's web. So far they had paid him very little attention, but McKenzie knew his time was coming.

Don Pedro's captain set a course for the marina at Puerto Banus. As they docked, McKenzie was untied from his spectator's chair and unceremoniously bundled into a cabin below deck. Still bound and gagged, he heard the door lock. They left him in a heap, face down on the Persian rug that smelled of camels, sand and Arabs…..

*   *   *

Miguel sailed out from La Carihuela and set his course for familiar fishing grounds in deeper water. He hoped not to snag a shark in his nets as he trawled the waters for sardines…..

16

McKenzie and the Digital Age

McKenzie was taken aback when the preacher walked up to the pulpit and said, "Please do not turn off your mobile phones. Leave them on and start texting and posting messages of what happens here to your friends on Facebook and Twitter. Attach photos and videos by all means."

Almost immediately, mobile phones being held aloft began flashing. Other phones were moving slowly as they panned the preacher and the congregation. "Be sure to invite the people you contact to come along to this meeting, if they can," said the preacher.

Before long, a stream of social network 'friends' began to stream into the meeting. Far from being distracting, the buzz was electrifying. The church was alive, the congregation was involved and the preacher was animated. There was some kind of activity going on everywhere.

All over the world, people were talking about the meeting that McKenzie was attending. Social networkers began to respond about what was happening in their own congregations, their home groups, whatever they were doing. Laughter and excited conversations began to ripple around the church.

Multimedia screens on the walls of the building began to relay images of the in-house meeting and of other meetings taking place at the same time all over the world. People, Christians and non-Christians, were uploading and broadcasting instantaneously. Churches were showing what was being uploaded online from a battery of multimedia projectors connected to laptops. Those with a Roku Box watched live streaming on their IP TVs.

The revelation hit McKenzie like a slap on the head; this was church and he loved it.

17

McKenzie is Hot

The car was warm, way too warm, and McKenzie was over-dressed. There had been a thick dawn mist that had rolled in from the sea and hung over the village all morning. Now, by mid afternoon, the mist had gone and the sun shone brilliantly in a cloudless blue sky. A quick scan of the people showed those who had been out-and-about since early morning; they were also overdressed. Purple overheated faces and flustered mothers milled to-and-fro with tantrum-throwing toddlers in their wake. Their, *I'm-not-giving-into-them-stare-straight-ahead* stance fooled no-one.

McKenzie opened his car door, being ever so careful not to bump the car parked next to his. Fresh, cool air flooded in. He took in a deep breath, filling his lungs to capacity and oxygenating his brain. He wedged his foot in the door to keep it open at a safe distance from his neighbour.

If the weather stayed good there would, no doubt, be a parade of scantily clad Scottish youth totally unashamed to show off their blue-white skin to the first decent rays of the year.

Was McKenzie going to have to wait much longer? He decided to step out of the car. As he stretched, he remembered another time in another place. However, this time there was no sound of a car backfiring in the steely cold, deserted streets of Moscow……

18

McKenzie Gets the Point

By the time McKenzie heard the key unlock the cabin door, he had manoeuvred himself into a sitting position on the floor with his back against the wall. At least that way he would see what was coming.

To his surprise, it was Maria who entered, unaccompanied. McKenzie looked her up and down. As usual, she was impeccably dressed with not even a hair out of place. Her dark eyes locked onto McKenzie's upturned face. He could detect no obvious signs of emotion other than absolute self confidence. She glided over to McKenzie and asked herself out loud, "What are we going to do with you?"

McKenzie, still gagged and bound, looked into Maria's face. She stooped, grabbed a corner of the duct tape that was over his mouth and gave it a good tug. McKenzie was now able to talk.

"Thank you", he said with a hint of cynicism while contorting his mouth and jaw.

"You're welcome", Maria responded with obvious sarcasm. "I want to hear you when you scream".

McKenzie was defenceless. His wrists were tied behind his back and his ankles bound together. Maria carefully positioned her expensively clad foot on McKenzie's groin and began pushing her pencil-thin stiletto into his crotch.

Maria's face broke into a crimson lip-gloss smile. "This will be such fun", she chuckled with perverse pleasure…..

*   *   *

As Miguel and his fishermen pulled their nets back onboard they knew that their catch was big. Their nets were heavy, but when they broke the surface they all stared horrified. There among the silvery sardines was a dead body, or at least what was left after

the sharks had finished….

19

McKenzie Hates Religion

The sound of the tolling bell invaded McKenzie's mind. It was seven a.m. on a sunny Sunday morning and the faithful were making their way to early mass.

Historically, France is a predominantly Roman Catholic country with a past that is steeped in religiosity far removed from the character of Jesus Christ. McKenzie believed that religion rooted in fear has bound and controlled many well meaning church-going Christians who, for the most part, are sadly unaware why they are so discontent in church.

McKenzie came from the Outer Hebrides of Scotland, a stronghold of religious control. He hated religion and that put him off Christianity although he didn't fully understand the difference between the two. Slowly, however, the revelation was beginning to dawn on him. McKenzie was soon to embark on a massive learning curve.

However, for the moment, McKenzie collected his thoughts and focussed on the day ahead. He knew that it contained potential dangers and he would need to have his wits about him. Emile, his long time friend, had set up the meeting with Youssef, a Moroccan refugee, who now earned a rather lucrative living by selling secrets to the highest bidder. He was not to be trusted.....

20

McKenzie is Amazed

As quickly as she had entered, Maria left the room, having caused relatively little damage. McKenzie was confused and wondered what was going on. Was this part of a psychological ploy to intimidate him?

Before McKenzie had a chance to work it all out, the cabin door swung open again and Maria stood, statuesque, framed in the doorway. She was dressed to kill in her bright red mini dress. Smoke rose from an extremely long cigarette delicately held in her perfectly manicured fingers.

"You intrigue me" she purred, toying with his mind and emotions. "I have been instructed to kill you for my pleasure, but before I do, I want to know who you are." McKenzie remained silent, giving nothing away.

"There is a smell from you that reminds me of my father back in Brazil. Maybe you are my father?" She let her question hang in the air. "I hate him! He abandoned me when I was a child." Maria's lip was quivering. "He didn't come to look for me when I was taken in the jungle."

McKenzie's mind raced back to twenty-five years ago when he had been part of a search party looking for a lost child deep in the Amazonian Rain Forest. Could it be?

"How come you have a Spanish name if you are from Brazil?" quizzed McKenzie at the risk of upsetting Maria still further. He hoped to lift a corner of the mystery that veiled Maria de las Flores' life.

"My captors took me to Colombia. Don Pedro wanted a daughter without the complications of a mother. He described exactly what he wanted and sent his men to find her. Unfortunately, his description matched me exactly and I became the daughter of the leader of Columbia's most feared drugs cartel. He renamed me and became my father …."

For the first time McKenzie saw Maria as that frightened little girl, lost and alone.

"You talk too much McKenzie!" hollered Maria, as she threw back her raven-black hair from her angry face and stormed out of the cabin. She was annoyed at allowing herself to open-up to someone she barely knew. It was that smell: bringing memories of her early childhood. She had not smelled it for twenty-five years…..

21

McKenzie and C.A.N.T

C.A.N.T. (Campaign Against Nuclear Terror), kept a fairly loose lead on their maverick agent McKenzie. He had the kind of relationship with CANT that James Bond enjoyed with the British Secret Service. However, the main difference between the two agents was that McKenzie didn't like martinis shaken or stirred.

McKenzie had built, over the years, a comprehensive portfolio of the world's nuclear terrorists: a 'Who's Who' of bad guys from all over the world. Now it was time to act. The clean-up operation would be global and extremely dangerous. These nuclear gangsters would fight to the death, making a nuclear war a very real threat.

Although they were spread around the planet, most of the key players knew or, at the very least, were familiar with each other. Nobody liked 'lone rangers' and, because of that, fly-by-night's didn't last long. They were a clandestine core group of shadowy figures who were disproportionately powerful for their number. Any one of them knew enough of the wrong people to blow the world apart.

McKenzie knew who they were and had met most of them face-to-face. That made him a target that not even CANT could protect….

22

McKenzie Goes Shopping

McKenzie pondered pensively on how best to avoid the inevitable. What a quandary! Online shopping was infested with dangerous predators of another kind. There was nothing else for it. He would stuff his ears with cotton wool, put on his bravest smile and, behind his clenched teeth, he would jolly-well grin and bear it....

Taking a deep breath, he stepped out onto yesterday's snow that crunched gingerly under his shifting weight. He caught the first bus heading towards the city centre. His brain was as numbed as the frozen monochrome landscape that underwhelmingly drifted past his almost opaque, dirty bus window. Cocooned in his own thoughts McKenzie's introvert bubble was about to burst...

As soon as he entered the mall, the sound of Christmas musak grated on McKenzie's jangled nerves. Every year it was the same old, same old. It was now official: McKenzie hated Wham and Slade!

It wasn't that McKenzie disliked Christmas; he had mixed feelings about it, but he most assuredly despised the overt commercial exploitation of it. This was not some Dickensian 'bah-humbug', rather it was, plain and simply, McKenzie's opinion based on his observations.

In conclusion, McKenzie loathed Christmas shopping. He didn't mind buying gifts for the people he loved but he detested being dragged into the bedlam that goes with it.

23

McKenzie comes out of Hibernation

McKenzie caught his reflection in a shop window. He couldn't believe what he saw. He looked like someone who had been isolated, hidden high on a mountain or deep in a jungle or lost in a desert. His eyes stared and darted everywhere, trying to make sense of too much information. He looked like a crazy-man, cowered and shuffling, as he looked for shadows to hide in.

His hair was long and so too was his beard. He was overweight and his clothes had seen better days. His reclusive lifestyle, whilst productive, had done nothing for his image. He was feeling fearful and overwhelmed among so many people in the city.

McKenzie needed a makeover, bad. First-off, he went for a short haircut and a beard trim. He wasn't ready to lose the beard altogether, he may need it to hide behind. He couldn't stomach the small talk from the slightly camp barber, he felt detached and uninvolved with his life and lifestyle.

McKenzie had been locked into his project all winter and he felt like a bear coming out of hibernation. In his mind, he had created a complex interweave of plots and intrigue and, in doing so, he had unwittingly distanced himself from the real world of 'ordinary' people. He was now struggling to re-connect.....

24

McKenzie Sub-Plot

Miguel radioed ahead informing the Coastguard and the Guardia Civil of his surprise catch. Before he reached the beautiful La Carihuela beach, he could see that it was packed with emergency service vehicles and, of course, the press.

Miguel ordered his small crew to unload the fish while the net, with the horrific human remains still entangled, was removed on a temporary winch set up on the sand. It was deposited into a screened off no-go area. Camera flashes popped and the TV cameras rolled, capturing every detail of the latest scoop.

The press scrum pushed microphones with their network logos attached, into Miguel's leathery face. He had seen many things during his forty-eight years of life but this took the biscuit. He was deeply affected by his grim catch. They asked him all kinds of questions....

"Where exactly were you fishing?"

"How long were you there?"

"How old is your boat?"

"What beer do you drink?"

Miguel, as he was advised by the police, declined to comment on anything.

The remains were officially photographed and catalogued then, with blue lights flashing and sirens wailing, they were rushed over to the mortuary where a detailed post mortem would take place. The media teams followed the ambulance in hot pursuit, each one looking for their own unique slant on this headline story.

Miguel was released after hours of questioning and told to stay local. At home, clearly shaken and shocked by his ordeal, he turned on his TV and there he was, on prime time national news, overseeing the removal of the remains from his boat and all the time saying, "No comment...."

* * *

Don Pedro was in a furious rage as he sat, incredulous, in front of his huge plasma screen on board La Dama de la Noche He had a few questions of his own to ask his buffoons and they better have good answers.....

25

McKenzie's Edge

During his time of self-imposed isolation, McKenzie had exercised less and eaten more. He had gained a few extra pounds. Not so much that anyone would notice, anyone that is, except McKenzie.

McKenzie felt that he had lost his edge. His mind was less sharp and his reactions were slow. He didn't like it, his keen instincts were fuzzy. It surely wasn't only as a result of being slightly overweight, although that would certainly contribute, no, there was something else. Isolation and a lack of interactive relationships would also be a factor. However, the one main cause for McKenzie being under par was directly related to McKenzie's distinct lack of adventure!

At heart, McKenzie was an adrenalin junkie and it had been far too long since his last fix. He was a man of action.

Now, with his project sufficiently advanced, it was time for McKenzie to start joining the dots. His first port of call was Pakistan. It was time to find out what was really going on with their nuclear arsenal…..

McKenzie's first meeting in Lahore didn't produce much although it was good to meet up with old friends. On his way to Multan, however, his driver detoured into Khanewal and things began to look up…..

26

McKenzie and the Mercedes

McKenzie waited anxiously for Maria to show. They had meticulously planned this meeting before she helped him to escape from 'La Dama de la Noche'. Maria had decided to go back to her real father in Sao Paulo, Brazil. Together with McKenzie, they had staged his escape and arranged a rendezvous in Marbella's Old Town.

McKenzie would drive them both, in his hired car, to Malaga Airport. They would catch a flight to London's Heathrow and, from there, onto Sao Paulo. Don Pedro would be so preoccupied with finding McKenzie that they should be absorbed into the populace of Sao Paulo before he even noticed that Maria was missing.

McKenzie had left some false trails that would, hopefully, lead Don Pedro into thinking that he had driven north to France. That was what McKenzie had loudly told the man at the car hire office in Puerto Banus.

McKenzie sat quietly outside 'La Gaviota' bar, drumming his fingers on the steering wheel of the hired black Merc and he waited……

27

McKenzie and the Lurking Danger

What's going on, mused McKenzie? The once familiar surroundings of his hometown, Glasgow were now strangely unfamiliar. The riverside area was completely transformed from the seedy haunts of unsavoury characters to a skyline that would rival downtown Manhattan.

As a student, McKenzie would often pass through the damp, dark and rundown side-streets of Anderston and the Broomielaw. Where low-budget prostitutes once loitered, there now stood chic, overpriced, luxury hotels and state-of-the-art office blocks.

McKenzie remembered the adrenalin-pumping thrill of lurking danger in sinister doorways. All that was now gone. The cosmopolitan city of Glasgow had become a mecca for culture vulture and a tourist attraction far removed from the territorial battlefields of razor-gangs in the 1950's. It had become a place to run to rather than from.

One thing hadn't changed however, the seedy underworld remained, hiding behind a façade of respectability and corporate success. There was still death on the streets, caused directly or indirectly, by the low-life pimps and pushers. McKenzie had a meeting scheduled with one of the worst of them.

Shaun, a descendent of Irish immigrants from a long line of navvies, had agreed to meet McKenzie in his penthouse suite at the top of the Hilton Hotel. The thrill of lurking danger came flooding back but this time it came dressed as psychopathic madman without a conscience. McKenzie was shaking.

Shaun, a notorious arms dealer supporting ideologies that massaged his ego, had information that McKenzie needed……

28

McKenzie Feels Vulnerable

To say Sanjid's house was shabby was a gross misunderstatement. The ancient outer edifice was crumbling and so too were the walls inside. It was highly unlikely that the windows had ever been cleaned. The threadbare linen curtains draped over them, although once vibrant with colour, were now sun-bleached to a monochromatic grey. They were held together by the cobwebs that generations of spiders had dexterously spun over gaping holes where countless flies were trapped in mass graves.

McKenzie stooped under the low roof in the dusty upstairs room where the meeting was to be held. Sanjid motioned for him to sit down, so McKenzie sat cross-legged on the warped wooden floor.

Sanjid had no desire to work in the brick factory that had employed his family since the day it was built. In an attempt to get out he had found himself a niche where he could run errands for the local underworld.

Unwittingly, he had found himself entangled with an Iranian-backed extremist group who, single-handedly wanted to rid Pakistan of every white infidel. McKenzie felt uncomfortable. Could he trust Sanjid? Could he trust Sanjid's friends who had brought McKenzie to the meeting?

Sanjid had information that was, potentially, worth a lot of money and that pay-off was his ticket to a better world far away from the political tensions and daily danger of living in Pakistan. He claimed to know of a secret arms dump that included a nuclear rocket silo. McKenzie knew that these guys were capable of committing any atrocity known to man (and a few that weren't!), even if that meant firing a nuclear bomb into any predominantly white country. They had neither morals nor scruples regarding mass murder or even single murder for that matter. McKenzie felt distinctly vulnerable…..

29

McKenzie on the Run

McKenzie grew increasingly more impatient as he waited in the Mercedes for Maria to show. It was now well past their pre-arranged rendezvous time. Maybe their plot had been discovered. If so, it was inevitable that Don Pedro's henchmen would extract all the details from her and then come for McKenzie. It would be safer for him to make his escape while he could but that would mean deserting Maria.

As he pondered this dilemma, framed in the car's rear-view mirror, his eye caught something moving in the shadows. His instincts kicked in and adrenalin exploded through his body. He threw himself out of the driver's door and ducked behind a large commercial refuse bin that had been wheeled out from 'La Gaviota' just moments earlier for the nocturnal bin-men.

A bullet ricocheted off the wall behind him. McKenzie, with lightning speed, gathered his thoughts. He positioned himself behind the large container and began to push it towards the gunmen. There was a slight downward slope on the road that helped McKenzie's barricade to gather momentum. The thick rubber bin easily absorbed the bullets that flew like hail in McKenzie's direction.

His shield came to an abrupt stop as it rammed into his assailants' 4x4 Range Rover. McKenzie took off down an alleyway like a stealth bomber, silently and with great speed, into the darkness and into the unknown….

30

McKenzie in the Cross-Fire

McKenzie never thought for a moment when he went to Tunisia that all hell would break loose. He had arranged to meet Aziz in Beni Khiar, a small town on the peripheries of the tourist trail that leads to Hammamet and not too far from the cosmopolitan city of Nabeul. It had seemed like a good idea to McKenzie to build in some rest and relaxation while he went about his business, under cover, as a tourist.

The newly built hotel was magnificently opulent and way under priced for its true value. Exhaling a slow sigh of contentment, McKenzie thought to himself, 'this is going to be so good....'

Almost overnight, like a shockwave from a huge political explosion, much of North Africa and the Arab Middle East erupted in civil unrest. The flashpoint was Tunisia. Unprecedented antigovernment riots brought chaos and destruction as a prelude to what would become unimaginable change.

McKenzie had to flee while he still could. He had to get out of Tunisia before the airports closed….

*   *   *

Later, from a safe haven in Paris, he had time to think. McKenzie was looking for answers. The biggest shift of global power since the fall of the Roman Empire had taken place suddenly. The stage was set, the demography of WMD was about to change forever.

What now? questioned McKenzie. In a very short space of time, the politics and balance of power in the Arab countries of North Africa and the Middle East had been revolutionised. Tyrannical dictators and corrupt governments had been replaced by rebel leaders who promised 'a time of change' for the good of the people. Where had he heard that before?

It all sounded like a hollow echo that had originated from the west. The prospect of these oil rich countries being governed by inexperienced young people, still high from their adrenalin-rush, sent warning signals to McKenzie. He sensed danger. Who would pull the strings?

The 'super powers', in fact, most countries around the world, recognised the authority of the victorious revolutionaries. However, would the new leaders be manipulated by outside powers eager to ally or, equally sinister, by hidden radicals from within….?

What would happen to the big weapons, the really big ones, the existing nuclear missiles or the ability to build them? McKenzie would need to tune into the jungle drums, to eavesdrop on who was talking and to whom……

31

McKenzie Gets Cooked

The wind died away leaving McKenzie sitting in the merciless inferno of airless sunshine. He felt like an experiment on oxygen deprivation. He focussed his mind and tried to find a place inside his head where he could cope. He tried not to sweat but beads of perspiration began to form on his forehead and he felt trickles of sweat run down his rib cage. There was nowhere to hide.

McKenzie's car, like McKenzie himself, had overheated on the sand-covered single-track road that ran from Reganne to In Salah through the Algerian Sahara. Wisely, he had a five-gallon drum of water in the back of his borrowed pick-up. McKenzie had turned off the engine to allow it to cool down. As he waited his mind went back to Spain and to Maria. She knew nothing of his whereabouts and, therefore, no amount of torture would make her give him away. He hoped that she would not suffer long before she died.

Vultures circled high overhead but McKenzie was determined that he was not going to become a carrion feast for them to gorge on. He popped the bonnet; there was a gentle hiss of steam as he opened the radiator cap. Bracing himself on the front bumper, he carefully began pouring water into the radiator. Immediately, it ran straight through, soaking his feet. The radiator was blown.

Stay calm, McKenzie told himself, there *is* a solution…..

32

McKenzie Goes Back to School

One day, out of the blue, a letter arrived inviting McKenzie to speak at his old school in Glasgow. They wanted him to speak about, 'The Secret Weapons of Mass Destruction'.

McKenzie had not been back to Glasgow Academy since he left in 1986. Memories came flooding back as soon as he entered the School Assembly Hall where he was to address the entire school, pupils and staff. McKenzie felt honoured.

Events that he had long forgotten returned with High Definition clarity. When he stood to the side of the podium waiting to be introduced, his eyes scanned the immaculately uniformed audience. There were more than thirteen-hundred pupils present.

McKenzie's mind flashed back to his third year at the school and to his first serious crush on the very beautiful Sarah Stewart.

She was as brilliantly academic as she was stunningly gorgeous. She had wavy raven-black hair that flowed over her shoulders and halfway down her back, her eyes were deep hazel pools of mystery and her flawless olive skin faultlessly complemented her petite and perfectly defined figure….

The sound of his name jolted McKenzie back to the present. He was introduced to the school as 'the leading expert in the clandestine world of secret weapons'. He waited for the applause to subside before he began…..

33

McKenzie has an Encounter

McKenzie sat bolt upright, his eyes popping. He was now completely awake but his 'dream' continued in vivid colour. There, in front of him, was a man, an incredibly handsome man, who seemed to emanate a brilliant bright light. His shoulder length hair was illuminated making it look like there was a halo around his head.

The light, although powerful, was not glary. It had a translucent effect that shimmered like a gossamer haze revealing the full spectrum of a magnificent rainbow arching around his unexpected visitor.

McKenzie felt elated, overwhelmed with joy. His guest's face shone with a broad friendly smile full of perfect white teeth. His eyes creased with laughter-lines.

'Peace be with you', he said, with a voice that sounded like a waterfall.

A wash of peace, unlike anything McKenzie had ever felt, flooded over him.

'I am your friend', he continued with the same beautiful voice.

Instantly McKenzie felt his heart melt and absolute trust mixed with tremendous gratitude gushed out of his innermost being. He had never felt such love for anyone or anything. McKenzie was transfixed.

'I am with you always'.

McKenzie believed it! He watched his friend's powerful arms open outwards. A kaleidoscope of colours spilled over McKenzie's upturned face. He knew that his new companion loved him enough to die for him. His heart beat so strongly that McKenzie thought it would burst. As he stared open-mouthed, his new best friend began to evaporate into an ethereal mist and disappear into the atmosphere that was pregnant with his presence.

McKenzie continued to stare into the empty space that had been temporally filled by the most glorious being he had ever seen. His mind could make no sense of it, but inside – deep inside, he knew he need never fear anything ever again. The sound of silence enveloped him as he slowly lay back down, his heart was still thumping inside his chest.

'Thank you', he said out loud to his friend. McKenzie was so overwhelmed he thought he would explode with joy.

'Thank you, McKenzie,' came the response, like a gentle whisper that carried him off into the most peaceful sleep he had ever known.

34

McKenzie Meets His First Love

When he had finished speaking at Glasgow Academy, over a cup of tea the Headmaster thanked McKenzie personally, and in the course of polite conversation happened to mention that the Annual Pupil's Reunion was about to take place in two week's time.

Trying not to appear too interested, McKenzie made a mental note of the details and began to let his mind wander. It was a long shot, a very long shot. Sarah Stewart could be anywhere with any one, not to mention children….

The day came and McKenzie decided to dress 'smart but casual'. As he dressed he couldn't help notice how nervous he was. 'Take a deep breath,' he told himself, 'relax'. This was ridiculous. The palms of his hands were sweating.

He helped himself to a courtesy drink when he entered and began to scrutinise the people who were gathering. What was he looking for? Sarah would probably have changed beyond all recognition. His eyes slowly roamed around the room stopping briefly at anyone who loosely fitted how she had looked twenty-five years ago.

Like a body blow from a prize fighter, the shock of instant recognition took his breath away. It was her, it was Sarah. Amazingly beautiful, her perfect teeth flashed pearly white behind her warm, charismatic smile. She was engaged in animated conversation with a group of young adults. One of them, who was both pretty and elegant, caught McKenzie's eye and came striding over to him.

'Dr McKenzie', she said respectfully, 'I had the honour of being at your talk to the school two weeks ago. It was marvellous. Please, I would love to introduce you to my friends'. Before he had time to think, McKenzie was being chaperoned across the room into the midst of the group he had been studying. 'These are my friends; Toby, Libby, Tom, Shelly and I'm Maggie. This is my mother.'

'Sarah', blurted McKenzie.

'Why, McKenzie!' smiled Sarah, 'where have you been hiding?'…..

35

McKenzie Finds Hope

McKenzie scanned the parched desert landscape expecting to see nothing, but hoping that he would see something or someone, some kind of life, anything. As his trained eyes journeyed slowly through the bleak, arid, inhospitable terrain, he stopped to look again at a speck in the distance. It hovered in the shimmering heat. It may have been his imagination, it may have been a mirage, but it was worth checking out.

McKenzie filled up his canteen with water from the drum in his pick-up and set off in the direction of that indistinguishable fragment of hope. As he got closer the speck grew larger and took on a distinct shape. When he finally reached it, McKenzie discovered with delight that he had stumbled upon a caravanserai: a roadside resting place where travellers could rest and recover from the day's journey. These caravanserai supported the flow, albeit sporadic, of commerce, information, and people across the network of trade routes throughout North Africa.

Although currently deserted, McKenzie knew that, eventually, some desert nomads or, perhaps, a travelling trader, would stop by for refreshment. All he had to do was wait…..

36

McKenzie is Shipwrecked

McKenzie slowly regained consciousness. He was lying face down in the sand. When he tried to move, every part of his body ached. What had happened, how did he get here?

His mind went back to the speedboat making directly for 'La Dama de la Noche', Don Pedro's luxury yacht. Don Pedro's men had caught up with McKenzie in Gibraltar where he had been attending a top-level, highly secretive meeting with military brass deep in the hollows of the Rock. When he stepped out of the black, chauffeured, diplomat's limo onto the steps of his hotel, Don Pedro's thugs had jumped him.

Hooded, bound and gagged, McKenzie was taken to 'La Dama de la Noche' where he was drugged and dumped below decks. After who knows how long and still fuzzy from the after-effects of the drugs, Don Pedro summoned McKenzie, unbound, to the fishing deck upstairs. While McKenzie had been unconscious below decks the yacht had left the marina and was now far out in open waters.

In an exaggeratedly benevolent voice, Don Pedro took delight in recounting the graphic details of how Maria had died: every gory detail. Now it was McKenzie's turn to die. McKenzie was very much on edge and his mind was working overtime as he desperately tried to hatch a plan for escape.

The sound of a racing engine distracted him. He looked into the distance and saw a small, white speedboat racing towards Don Pedro's opulent cruiser. There was a sudden moment of panic interrupted by an almighty explosion as the speedboat slammed into the side of 'La Dama de la Noche'.

'It must have been crammed full of explosives', thought McKenzie just before everything went dark…..

37

McKenzie and the Smell

It was the smell that first caught McKenzie's attention. It transported him back to a time when he lived in Kisumu, Kenya. He was six years old.

His family lived in the security of the military compound where his father had been unexpectedly stationed. McKenzie made friends quickly with some of the other white children, but it was the Kenyan children that he liked the most. He had never known any black kids before.

Blessing was a boy roughly the same age as McKenzie, but that's where the similarities stopped. Blessing had a younger sister called Precious. Together they came into the compound every day. While their mother cleaned around the compound her children would sit, well behaved, on the carefully tended lawn.

When it came time to clean McKenzie's family home, McKenzie would go out to play. Blessing loved football and so too did McKenzie. They didn't speak each other's language but football knew no language barriers. During the rough and tumble of close-contact hot and sweaty games, McKenzie noticed the fresh smell of eau de toilette. Blessing's mother must have splashed it on her children to keep them smelling fresh in the hot African sunshine.

As soon as the family sat next to him on the plane he smelled it: that same clean, fresh smell. They must have been rushing to catch their flight; a mother, her two children and, McKenzie presumed, a family friend. He breathed deep and enjoyed the memories that the smell evoked…..

38

McKenzie Tames a Scream

McKenzie felt decidedly uncomfortable. He was twitchy and he was agitated. A quiet scream began to form deep inside him. He had to get out of there, now!

A combination of last night's over-indulgence and the droning monotone of a serious contender for the world's most unmotivational speaker gave McKenzie an insatiable desire to escape.

Boardrooms were among McKenzie's least favourite places to be. The complex interweave of personalities, megalomaniac egos and secret agendas filled the room like the stench from an open sewer.

The scream within him was about to burst out, but McKenzie had to tame it and remain silent. It was for the greater good of the cause. How else was he ever going to see a difference made to the plight of the untold multitudes of abandoned, marginalised and forsaken people who were lost in a savage world that was not their own?

McKenzie was moved with such deep compassion at the condition of those less fortunate than himself. He was absolutely passionate about doing all that he could to help them. He was on the Board of Directors of some large charities but it was the little, less well known NGO's, that he really wanted to help most. Those that weren't afraid to get their hands dirty, those that moved in close-up-and-personal and got in among the people they wanted to help.

Today, he was flying the flag for *'Make a Change'*, a little-known feeding charity that provided meals for school age children in the world's poorest places. McKenzie wanted to do all he could to help them. He waited his turn to speak and when he did, he shot from the hip. Money, not manners, were what was needed most....people were dying because of political correctness. It was time for action, now!

39

McKenzie the Warrior

To McKenzie they looked like giant claymore-wielding warriors; to others they were wind turbines that revolved majestically in lines across the undulating hills of the Southern Uplands of Scotland.

In a bygone era, ferocious warriors would have lined these same hills; tartan-clad armies that fought face-to-face with every invader. The Scots were fearless, even wild, and they were feared by every adversary who came against them. Throughout history, from the Picts until now, Scottish soldiers were infamous in battle.

McKenzie had a fighting spirit, a warrior spirit. He was as tenacious as a West Highland Terrier and he was a champion of his cause to oppose the use of nuclear terrorism. He was respected by both good and bad alike.

Now was the time to pull from his Scottish DNA, to summon every ounce of courage he could muster. The al-Qaeda Jihadists had progressively infiltrated Pakistan from the north. They had caused carnage among the tribal factions and, through a carefully planned strategy of bombings and kidnappings, they had brought fear and terror among the placid Pakistanis.

They had usurped the power of the Pakistani government and used them as a façade to hide behind. They had gained control of the Pakistani defence systems and al-Qaeda now had full nuclear capability.

McKenzie knew exactly what was going on, he drew his intel from the darkest inside sources. Al-Qaeda intended to fire a nuclear bomb and the target was London. This news hadn't hit the media yet and that gave McKenzie a small window of opportunity before the panic started…..

40

McKenzie Finds a Diamond

McKenzie found a diamond, and a rough diamond at that. Dale was precious and he didn't even know it. With a little spit and polish he could become a very valuable asset to McKenzie's mission.

Dale was smart, but he was also innocent, almost to the point of being naïve. He could learn all that McKenzie had to teach him. On top of all that, McKenzie liked him even if he was a little quirky.

He would invite Dale to accompany him on a couple of trips and he would teach him by example. McKenzie was excited; he could sure use help and Dale was it! Just lately McKenzie had felt exhausted; worn-out and frazzled. Young blood, that's what he needed.

Mexico was already on McKenzie's radar, Dale would love it and McKenzie felt sure he would rise to the challenge…..

41

McKenzie Finds Some Shade

Even on the promenade, *el paseo maritimo*, in Fuengirola, there was hardly a breath of air. Not even a sea breeze. McKenzie sat on a bench under the sparse shade of a sapling orange tree.

He marvelled at the hoards of foreign holiday makers laid out on towels along the beach like meat on a barbeque griddle. They turned themselves over to get thoroughly cooked. Their skin tones ranged from raw pink to well done.

It was two o'clock in the afternoon and McKenzie remembered that only mad dogs and Englishmen went out in the mid-day sun. He was here to meet Miguel, the fisherman who had worked in *La Carihuela* at the time when he pulled up in his nets what was left of Don Pedro's ex-Columbian overseer, Paco. That was a while ago.

Don Pedro had sent Miguel a gift that he couldn't refuse. He told him to keep the details of his surprise catch suitably vague. With that money Miguel had bought a bigger fishing boat and he now sailed out of Fuengirola's fishing port. McKenzie had arranged to meet Miguel in one of the expensive yacht club bars at the other side of the port.

McKenzie made his way there, thinking it should be quiet at this time of the day……

42

McKenzie Plunges into Darkness

McKenzie was spiralling backwards, falling into empty darkness. He felt helpless; unable to coordinate his movements; unable to think straight. What was happening to him? He had no idea.

He reached out desperately, trying to catch hold of something, anything to stop him falling. He grabbed at something horrible and slimy that gave him the creeps but it slipped from his grasp.

As it slipped from his grasp, McKenzie saw the ugliest face of indescribable evil stare back at him. It had piercing dark eyes that gripped his soul. Panicking, McKenzie scanned the unyielding void. At that moment the screaming started: eerie, spine-chilling, blood-curdling screaming, first one demented, twisted voice then another and another.

The cacophony was overwhelming; ear-splitting, unrelenting like slow sadistic torture to the point of death but death, like a predator, toyed with its prey.

Spinning, spiralling deeper, McKenzie plummeted downwards into the gaping jaws of whatever awaited him in the chasm below…..

43

McKenzie Fans the Flame

It had been three days since the school reunion. McKenzie had hardly slept a wink. Every time he thought about Sarah, his heart skipped a beat. She had readily agreed to meet McKenzie for coffee in a city centre café in the heart of the, now fashionable, Merchant City area of Glasgow.

McKenzie had discovered that Sarah had been widowed by a freak accident that caused her husband's single-engine light aircraft to crash, killing him instantly. That was seven years ago.

Sarah had raised Maggie single-handedly while working as a research scientist in the labs attached to Strathclyde University. Maggie, having just finished her exams, was about to become a student at Strathclyde Uni where she hoped to study and to follow in her mother's footsteps.

McKenzie felt like a young boy again, besotted and head-over-heels in love. He wanted, above all things, to wrap his arms around Sarah and squeeze her close to himself. He wanted to kiss her luscious red lips, but he would have to wait.

Firstly, he had to find out how Sarah felt about him….

44

McKenzie Builds a Den

As a child, McKenzie loved his hiding places or 'dens' as he called them: a Scottish word presumably derived from the word 'hidden'. He could climb into his den, into his imaginary world, and be lost in wonder for days.

As an adult, McKenzie still loved to hide away from time to time. He had a network of dens all over the world. He had one deep in the Amazonian Rain Forest of Brazil and he had another in Ogembo, a town of little consequence in Western Kenya.

When he was a child, around the age of six, McKenzie had lived in Kisumu, in a military compound, with his parents. Ever since then he had a soft spot in his heart, filled with happy memories, of the people and the place.

His boyhood friend Blessing's grandfather had died, leaving his house in the countryside of Ogembo, empty. The distance from Kisumu to Ogembo was a little over eighty miles, so McKenzie bought it. It was a *Nyamwezi*, a circular building with walls made of mud and cattle dung. It had one solitary low door, a little window and a thatched roof. It wasn't much to look at but it was McKenzie's Kenyan den.

Ogembo was a market town where most of the surrounding farmers sold their produce. It was close to the equator and it rained a lot giving it a warm, tropical climate. The land was fertile producing mostly white maize and tea.

McKenzie loved to live like a native when he was in Ogembo. However, he kept himself to himself, preferring solitude to socializing. He knew the locals and they knew him. He thought he knew their primitive ways until, one day unannounced, a stranger turned up......

45

McKenzie and the Yacht Club

As McKenzie waited for Miguel to show, he nursed an iced diet coke and allowed his eyes to drift over the bobbing boats moored in front of him; big yachts, cabin cruisers, modest boats for sale and ostentatious beauties that would cost millions of Euros.

Overly loud laughter and cockney accents caught his attention. McKenzie couldn't make out their words but he could pick up the brash vibe of Costa criminals revelling in exaggerated stories from their shared past.

McKenzie knew from experience that they weren't swapping stories of recent criminal activities. They would more likely be sharing anecdotes of past exploits and prison sentences, having a laugh at triumphs and failures involving the criminal fraternity that they all knew.

This wouldn't be loose talk, no, careless talk cost lives and that life could be yours! McKenzie knew that this strip of coastline from Torremolinos to Marbella was a favoured hide-out for foreign criminals and a hallowed haven for cooling off after a big job.

McKenzie felt uncomfortable just being within earshot. He hoped Miguel would show soon…..

46

McKenzie in the Mountains

Ensconced in the Himalayas of Northern Pakistan, McKenzie, in a vain attempt to cut out the draughts and beat back the deadly cold, wrapped himself tightly in the inadequate blanket he had been given.

He was in this bombed-out hell hole to meet the al-Qaeda leaders who had wreaked havoc on the unsuspecting infidels of the west. Hiding out in a network of underground caves, this little group of terrorist extremists had masterminded the worst Machiavellian acts of evil since the Gestapo of the Second World War.

McKenzie had managed to secure a meeting with them only days before their planned attack on the city of London. He hoped to dissuade them from 'pressing the button' with offers of power and influence within the Pakistani government. Oh yes, this they already had albeit illegally, but McKenzie hoped that the offer of recognised status from many of the World Powers would sway them.

They treated McKenzie with respect, they knew who he was but McKenzie would have to offer them a lot more than recognition. The Al-Qaeda leaders had set their sights high, they wanted status and a land and a nation of their own. How this could ever be given was impossible to imagine. Al-Qaeda, also known as the International Islamic Front for Jihad against the Crusaders and the Jews, made their fight with everyone who is not on their side.

McKenzie's main task was to dissuade them from using their WMD. Getting them to lay them down would require a miracle. The ultimate aim of al-Qaeda is to destroy America by bringing about its economic collapse. They aim to do this by goading them into a 'War on Terror' in a variety of Muslim countries. In doing so, al-Qaeda hopes to drain the USA economy.

The strain of multiple engagements in numerous places would make the worldwide economic system, dependant on the USA dollar, also collapse and that would lead to global political instability. In turn, this will ultimately lead to a worldwide jihad led by Al-Qaeda. Their ideal, after that, would be to establish an ultra conservative form of Islamic government to rule across the world.

If ever McKenzie needed to pray, it was now....

47

McKenzie is Diverted

As McKenzie carefully made his way back to his seat from the toilet, he was aware that the sleeping passengers with upturned, open-mouthed faces didn't notice that the turbulence was getting stronger. McKenzie was almost thrown into his seat. The 'fasten seatbelts' sign lit up and the cabin crew announced that it was necessary for all passengers to return to their seats to ride out the storm. Lightning flashed outside the window. It lit up the heavy rain and the angry black clouds…..then another flash.

This time McKenzie saw the fork lightning hit the wing of the plane. The reassuring voice of the pilot calmly told everyone onboard the 737 that one of the starboard engines had been 'immobilised' by the storm and the plane was being forced to make an emergency landing at the next airport, Cincinnati.

A wave of panic broke over every passenger who was awake, incredulously some continued to sleep completely undisturbed by the raging storm and potential danger.

Cincinnati was not where McKenzie was heading. His contact in Detroit would have to wait until his next connecting flight.....

48

McKenzie in the Light

The smell of sulphur and the stench of filth made McKenzie want to retch. It overpowered him; dank, putrid decay, the reek of death. The tortured screaming was at fever-pitch way beyond the capabilities of anything human.

Involuntarily, McKenzie let out a scream himself. It came from somewhere deep within and inside that desperate cry was every ounce of McKenzie's last hope of survival.

Out of nowhere McKenzie suddenly felt his fall being cushioned by an invisible source. Instead of falling downwards into the jaws of the devouring black evil abyss he was travelling upwards at the speed of light towards a glorious, magnificent, iridescent interweave of brilliant colours. McKenzie was exhilarated, he was overwhelmed with euphoria. Elated and filled with tremendous joy, McKenzie lay back into the invisible arms and enjoyed the ride.

All of a sudden, McKenzie was in the centre of an inexpressible light. Colours flashed all around him. He could almost touch and taste each colour. However, as he reached out to take hold of them they morphed into yet another holographic display of tremendous beauty.

Peace began to soak him like mist on a mountainside; like a breath. A gentle breeze caressed him in love. McKenzie didn't want it to stop. He thought that his heart would burst with such tremendous elation, a symphony of love, joy and peace. Still it came, wave after wave of enrapturing harmony.

McKenzie felt at one with all that was happening. He blended into the light and the love until he was completely unaware of himself. He knew that he had been saved from utter, unending evil and he was now soaked and saturated in this expansive, great goodness. He didn't want it to stop and somehow, deep inside, he

knew it never would…..

49

McKenzie and the Unscheduled Stop Over

Due to the quiet two-o'clock-in-the-morning roads, the bus that took the disgruntled passengers from Cincinnati Airport to the hotel (courtesy of Delta Airlines) made good and comfortable progress on the twenty miles journey. There were only fifteen people who had to sleep-over on account that there was no late night flight from Cincinnati to Detroit.

Bleary-eyed but resigned to the necessity of the unscheduled stop-over, McKenzie casually perused his fellow passengers. His eyes stopped to take a second look at a certain Asian passenger. McKenzie couldn't be certain but he thought he recognised him from a recent visit he had made to Northern Pakistan. Surely not, it couldn't be?

Once in his room, McKenzie typed-in his password and activated the fingerprint recognition on his laptop. He opened up the encrypted file containing details of his recent trip to Pakistan and, there he was, Ashar Abdul Sohail.

Asher had been flagged-up as someone to watch as a potential threat to the delicate balance of power between the insurgent terrorists and the western allies who, at any cost, would do everything possible to prevent terrorist activities on their home turf. McKenzie flipped open his secure mobile phone and made a call to Captain Stein of Homeland Security….

50

McKenzie and the Toilet Brush

McKenzie stretched himself like an old dog getting up after a long sleep in front of an open fire. His bones cracked but it felt good. McKenzie had been sat in front of his PC for far too long. He took a big drink of his cool*ish* diet coke, burped, broke wind and went to the toilet. He thought he was in the flat on his own but he wasn't....

Through the space under the toilet door McKenzie was sure that he saw a shadow moving; no sound but a shift of light. He was convinced that someone was waiting to attack him outside the door.

McKenzie looked around for something that he could use as a weapon. All he could see was a toilet brush. It was fairly sharp at the end of the handle but it would be no use against a gun or a knife.

Quietly, he pulled up his pants and remembered not to flush the toilet thus signalling his imminent exit. Fortunately, the door opened outward and McKenzie pushed it open as fast and as hard as he could. His assailant was behind the door and, much to McKenzie's satisfaction, it thumped hard against him.

The poker in his assailant's hand bounced off the hall carpet. Mr Jeffrey staggered backwards dazed and with a bleeding nose. Poor old Mr Jeffery, McKenzie's kind-hearted next-door-neighbour. Believing the house was empty, he was suspicious when he saw the light on in McKenzie's study. That would teach him to stick his (now bleeding) nose into someone else's business.

No real harm was done and soon the neighbour's were best friends again. They had a good laugh at their own, somewhat pathetic, attempt at heroics, slowly shaking their heads like two nodding dogs on the parcel shelf of a family car. They smiled as they reminisced over a cup of tea. 'There had been a time…. and it seemed like only yesterday', mused Mr Jeffrey. McKenzie, now far away in another place with his own thoughts, said nothing….

Comments

'Pure Genius!' Robert Bruce Chief Petty Officer Royal Navy Submariner - Scotland

'Am I McKenzie?' Pamela Taylor Beauty Therapist - Scotland

'The vision of Jesus is brilliant, praying in tongues brilliant and I loved the chapter about McKenzie's den in Kenya.' Katharine Baumanis palliative care nurse – Australia

'Excellent! I thoroughly enjoyed it all. Vivid descriptions and memorable locations from all around the globe.' Thomas Thomson Student - Scotland

'McKenzie is profound! I am moved to tears at several points, not because the action is emotional, but rather the content and questions and his wonderings resound in all of us. This is from God, I am so sure of it. For those that want to know Him and bypass the doctrinal sludge that tends to weigh us down, McKenzie is perfect.

Several years ago, a military drama premiered on silver screens across the world in which one line has become notorious for making the movie. In the famous courtroom scene, a lawyer

slams his fist on the table while yelling at the defendant, "I want the truth." In much the same way, I see believers around the world slamming their spiritual fist on a table demanding to know the truth. I know because I was one of them. I grew up in church but failed to know, really know, God. It is my prayer that as you read Who Is McKenzie?, your eyes will be opened, the truth revealed, and for the impact of that truth to reach forward into generations to come. Whether you need to wipe your slate clean as I did, or to hear the message for the first time, I believe Peter will profoundly affect the way you view God. For those that want to know Him and bypass the doctrinal sludge that tends to weigh us down, McKenzie is perfect.' Mary Nichelson Editor, journalist, talk show host – USA

CONTACT DETAILS

Kilcreggan House, Kilcreggan G84 0JT Scotland

http://www.peterstanwaybooks.com

ALSO AVAILABLE FROM PETER STANWAY

'Wee Boys from Glasgow Don't Cry'

An autobiographical real life story of personal transformation

Wee Boys from Glasgow Don't Cry is a challenging real-life roller-coaster story of survival and victory. In the twilight zone of drugs and alcohol, Peter spirals deeper into a desperate lifestyle with no holds barred. On the run with another man's wife, extreme personal transformation is just about to hit him! Completely dysfunctional from years of hedonism he is thrown a lifeline from where he last expected. With no options left, Peter grabs the outstretched hand of Jesus. The power of God knocks him to the floor. When he gets up he is totally changed. The real adventure is about to begin …..

Buy from PeterStanwayBooks.com

This book is also available wherever and however books are sold

ISBN 0-9772194-4-5
ISBN13 978-0-9772194-4-5

Lightning Source UK Ltd.
Milton Keynes UK
UKOW020616091211

183472UK00001B/5/P